Super Minds

Workbook Starter

Herbert Puchta Günter Gerngross Peter Lewis-Jones

	Hello	2		On the farm	58
1	My classroom	8	7	I'm hungry!	68
2	My family	18	8	All aboard!	78
3	My face	28	9	Party clothes	88
4	Toys	38		Cut-outs	99
5	My house	48			

CAMBRIDGE
UNIVERSITY PRESS

Hello

1 **Match and say the names.**

1 Trace and match.

1 ^{CD1} **06** **Listen and trace.**

1

2

3

4

4 I'm (Mike, Leo, Gina, Polly).

Think! **Look and colour.**

1

2

1 **Colour. Say the words.**

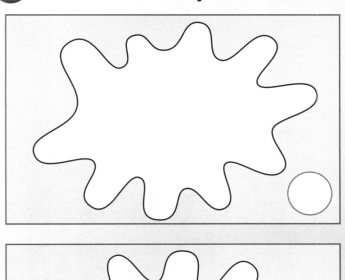
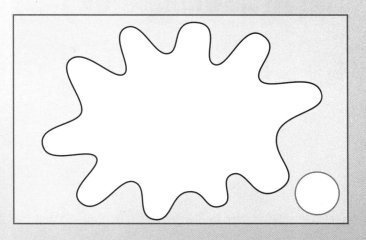
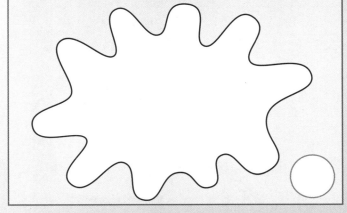
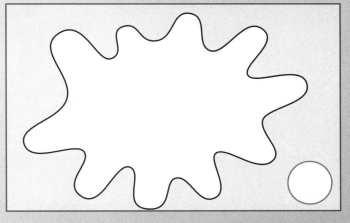
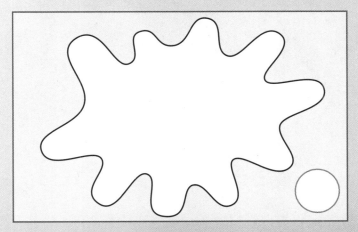

2 **Draw faces.** ☺ ☺ ☹

1 My classroom

Find and colour.

pencil, chair, bag, rubber, book, desk

1 CD1 14 **Listen and circle.**

1
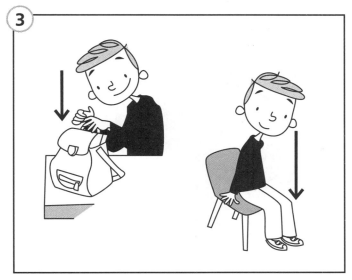

2

3

4

5

6

Stand up. Sit down. Open ... Close ... Pick up ... Put ...

1 Draw and colour.

1 Think! **Count and match.**

1 2 3 4 5 6

Listen and trace.

 1      

 2      

3      

4      

Think! **Look and colour.**

1

2

1 CD1 21 **Listen and colour. Colour to match.**

1

2

3

4

5

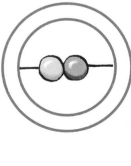

1 Look and circle.

1

2

3

4

5

Make a collage.

This is us!

1 Say the words. Colour the circles.

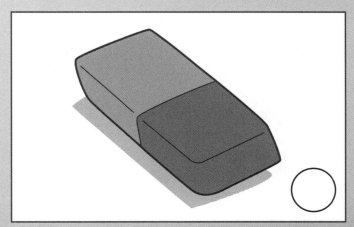 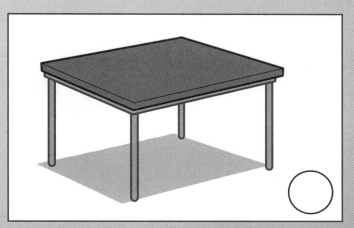

2 Draw faces.

2 My family

1 Circle and say the words.

18 grandpa, grandma, mum, dad, sister, brother

1 Listen and circle.

1

2

3

4

5

6

This is my (brother), (Tom). 19

1   Point and say the names and the words.

①

②

③

④

⑤

⑥

1 **Draw lines. Colour and make sentences.**

1      

2      

3   

4      

Think! Look and colour.

1

2

1 Look and draw.

1 Think! Look and say the family words.

1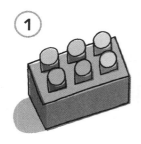

2

3

4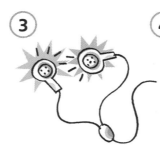

5

1 **Make an ice lolly stick family.**

1 Say the words. Colour the circles.

 ○

 ○

 ○

 ○

 ○

 ○

2 Draw faces. ☺ 😐 ☹

 ○

 ○

 ○

3 My face

1 **Colour the clown.**

2 **Describe your clown. Colour your friend's clown.**

eyes, ears, nose, face, teeth, mouth

1 Think! Look, draw and say the words.

How are you feeling today? Complete the face.

 **Listen and circle.**

1

2

3

4

Are you (angry)? Yes, I am. / No, I'm not. 31

Listen and trace.

1 (Think!) Look and colour.

1 Think! Join the dots and answer.

1

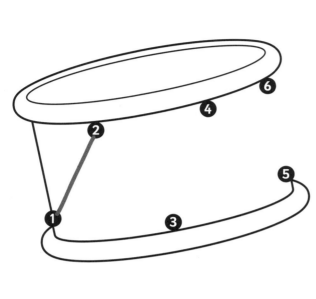

2

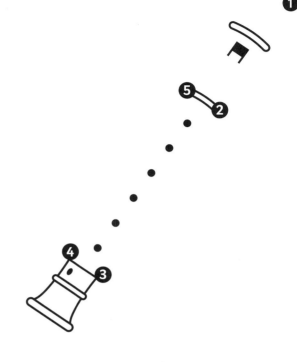

3

4

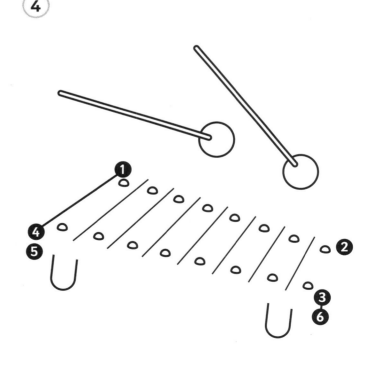

Think! **Look and draw.**

1 Make a xylophone.

1 Say the words. Colour the circles.

 ○

 ○

 ○

 ○

 ○

 ○

2 Draw faces.

4 Toys

1 **Think!** Count and match.

1 2 3 4 5 6

ball, kite, rope, teddy bear, doll, plane

1 **Draw four toys.**

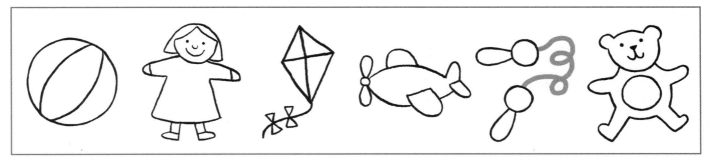

2 **Describe your picture. Draw your friend's picture.**

1 **Complete the toys. Draw the missing toy.**

1 CD1 53 **Listen and colour.**

2 Think! **Count and draw.**

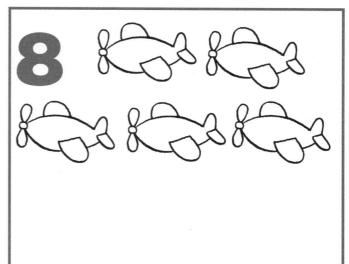

1 CD1 55 Listen and trace.

1

2

3

4

1 **Think!** **Look and colour.**

1

2

Look and draw two ropes and three balls.

 **Think!** Look and circle red and blue .

1 Make a paper plane.

1 **Say the words. Colour the circles.**

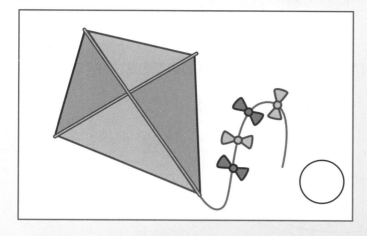 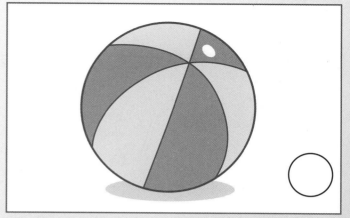

2 **Draw faces.** ☺ ☺ ☹

5 My house

1 **Think!** **Match, colour and make sentences.**

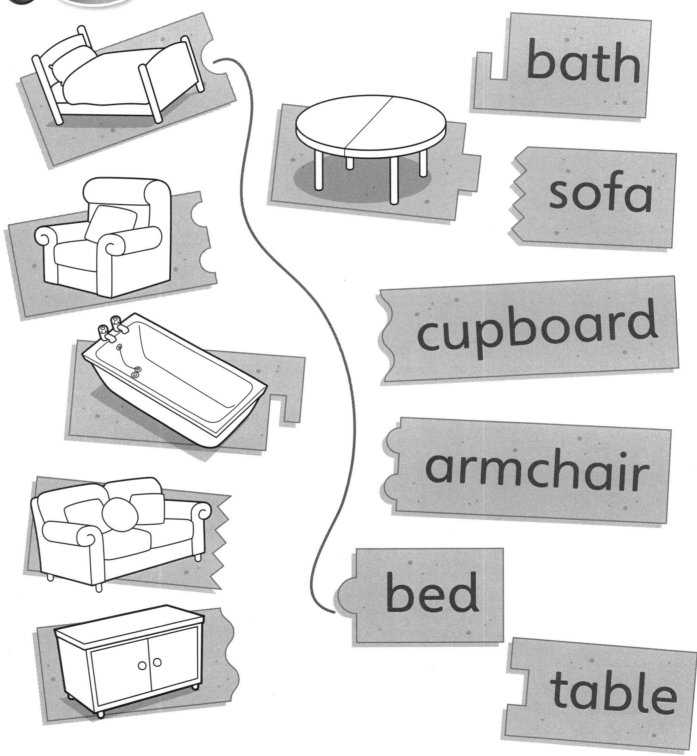

bath

sofa

cupboard

armchair

bed

table

bath, cupboard, bed, sofa, table, armchair

1 **Listen and circle.**

1 **Draw lines.**

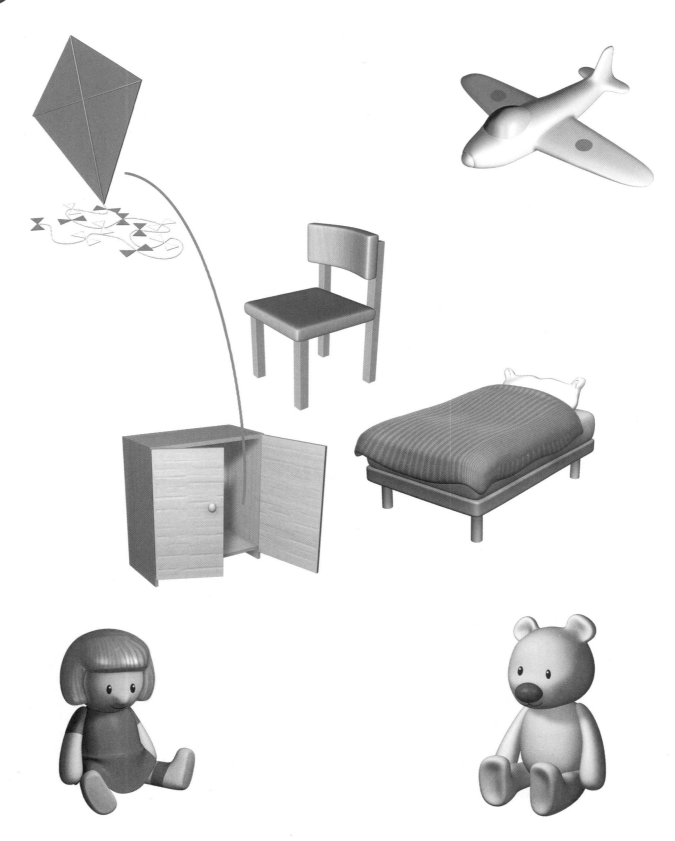

1 Find pairs and circle.

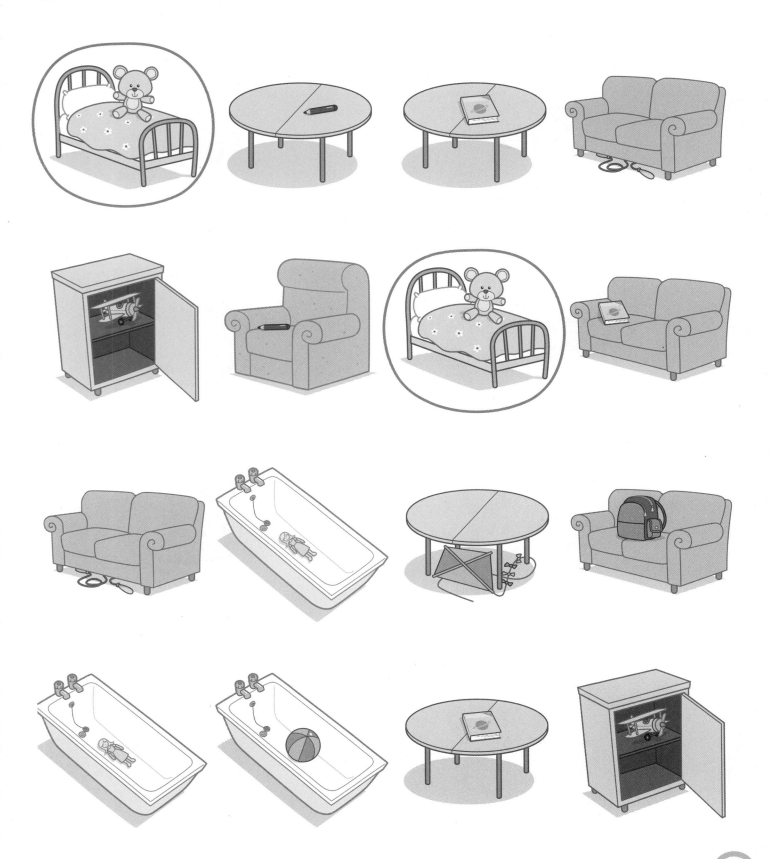

The (doll) is (in) the (bath). 51

Listen and trace.

1

2

3

4

1 Think! Look and colour.

1

2

1 Listen and colour.

1	2	3	4	5	6

2 Think! Look and colour.

Think! Follow the path. Count and circle.

|  | 1 | 2 | 3 | 4 | 5 | 6 | 7 | 8 | 9 | 10 |

1 Make dolls' furniture.

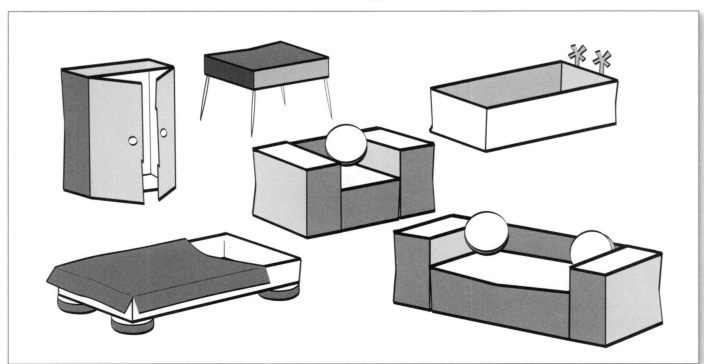

5

1 **Say the words and trace. Colour the circles.**

bed ◯

table ◯

armchair ◯

cupboard ◯

sofa ◯

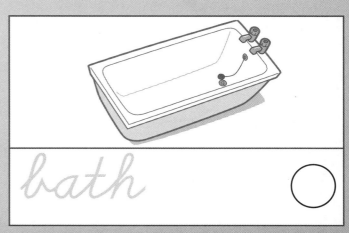

bath ◯

2 **Draw faces.** ☺ 😐 ☹

 ◯

 ◯

 ◯

6 On the farm

1 **Complete the animals. Say the words.**

①

dog

②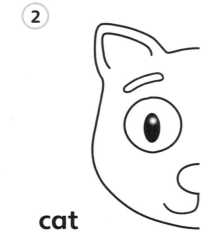

cat

③

sheep

④

cow

⑤

rabbit

⑥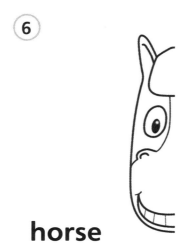

horse

1 **Draw your favourite animals.**

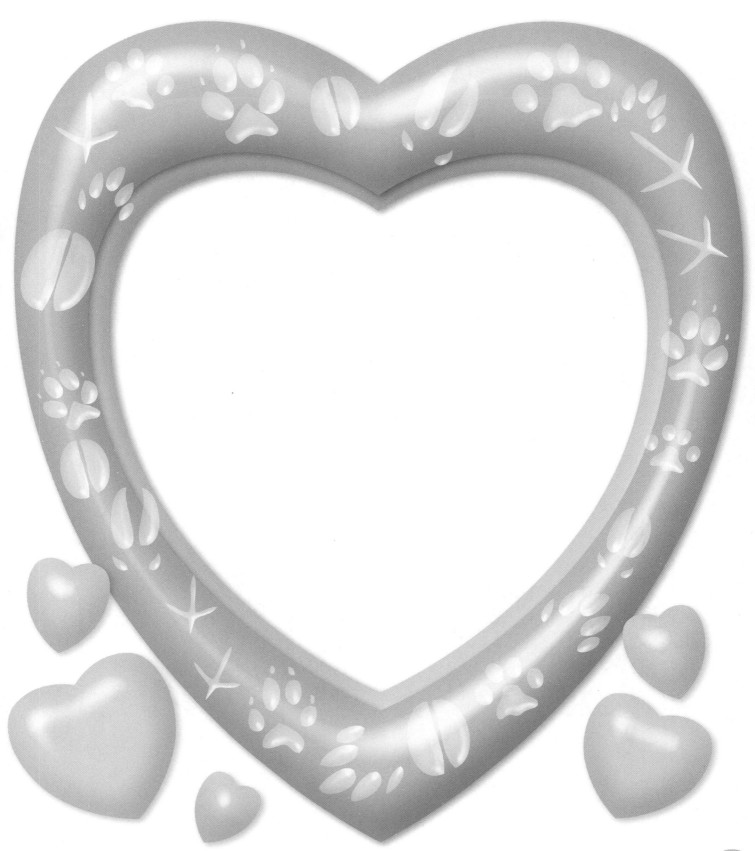

(two) sheep, three (cat)s, I like (cats) 59

1 Listen, point and say the words.

1 CD2 20 Listen and colour. Follow the paths.

My favourite colour is (blue) / (toys) are (planes).

1 CD2 22 **Listen and trace.**

1

2

3

4

1 **Think!** Look and colour.

1

2

1 **Match. Where do they live?**

1 Think! Look and cross out.

1 Make a woolly sheep.

6

1 **Say the words and trace. Colour the circles.**

dog ◯

cat ◯

sheep ◯

cow ◯

rabbit ◯

horse ◯

2 **Draw faces.** ☺ ☺ ☹

 ◯

 ◯

 ◯

7 I'm hungry!

1 Think! **Look, draw and say the words.**

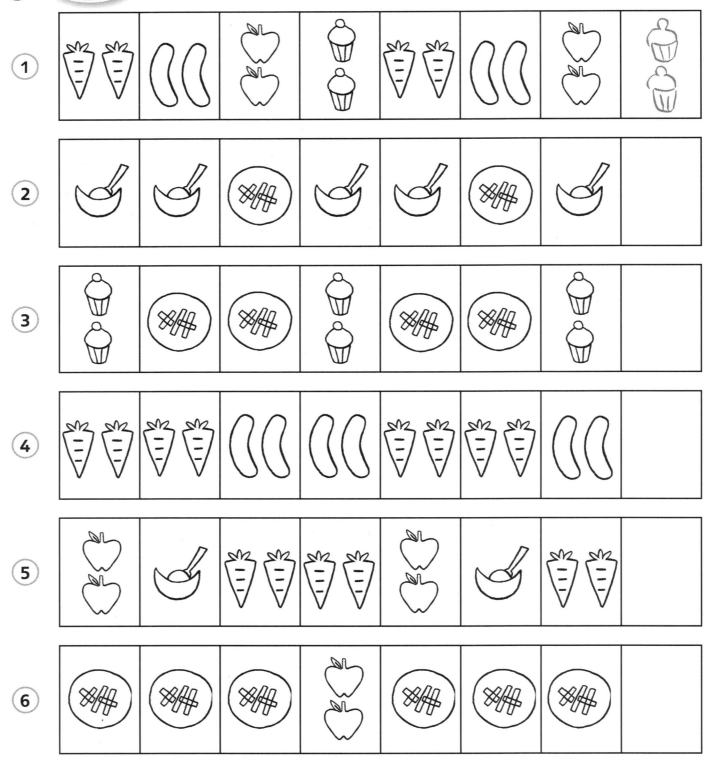

carrots, sausages, apples, cakes, ice cream, chips

1 Listen and match.

CD2 28

2 Draw your favourite food.

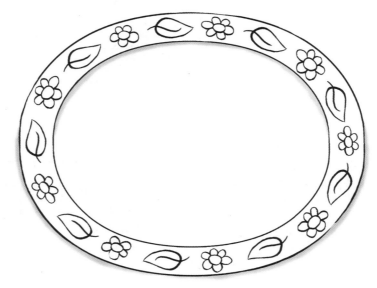

1 Draw.

1 **Draw faces.** ☺ ☹ **Tell your friend and draw.**

chips		
sausages		
cakes		
carrots		
ice cream		
apples		

1 CD2 32 **Listen and trace.**

①

②

③

④

1 Think! Look and colour.

1

2

Value: don't be greedy   73

1 Draw lines. Describe the meals.

Think! **Look and circle.**

1

2

3

4

1 **Make biscuit faces.**

1

2

3

4

1 **Say the words and trace. Colour the circles.**

carrots ◯

sausages ◯

apples ◯

cakes ◯

ice cream ◯

chips ◯

2 **Draw faces.** ☺ ☒ ☹

 ◯

 ◯

 ◯

8 All aboard!

1 Think! **Match, colour and make sentences.**

car

bike

scooter

bus

boat

train

boat, train, car, scooter, bus, bike

1 Follow the lines. Make sentences.

1 Listen, point and say the words.

1 **Think!** **Listen and circle.**

1

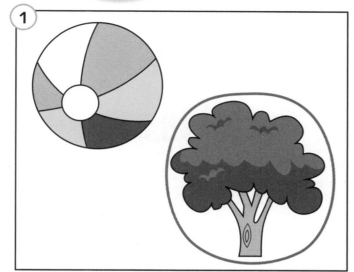

2

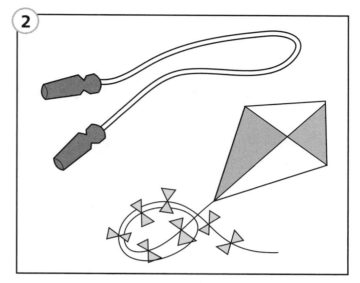

3

4

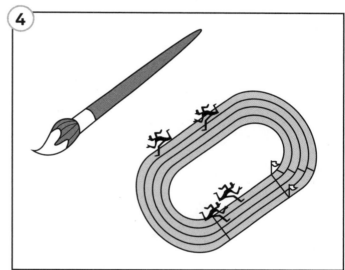

5

6

flying a kite, swimming, climbing a tree, running, brushing my teeth, washing my hands

1 **CD2 44** **Listen and trace.**

①

②

③

④

1 Think! **Look and colour.**

1

2

1 Trace with four colours to match.

2 Draw and say the shapes. □ △ ▭ ○

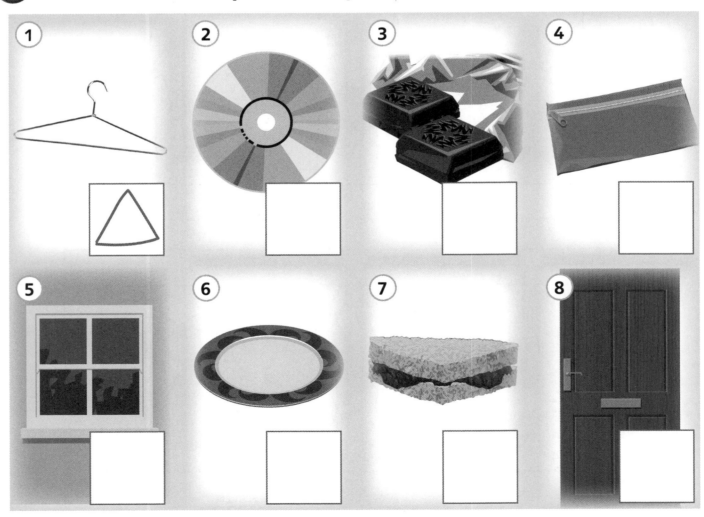

1 **Think!** **Count and circle.**

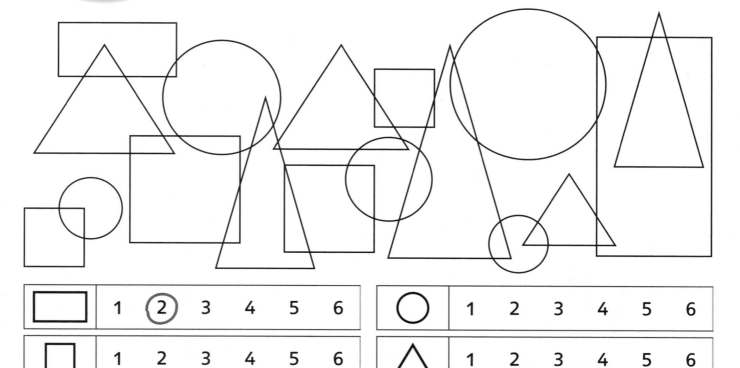

▭	1	②	3	4	5	6

◯	1	2	3	4	5	6

☐	1	2	3	4	5	6

△	1	2	3	4	5	6

2 **CD2 46** **Listen and colour.**

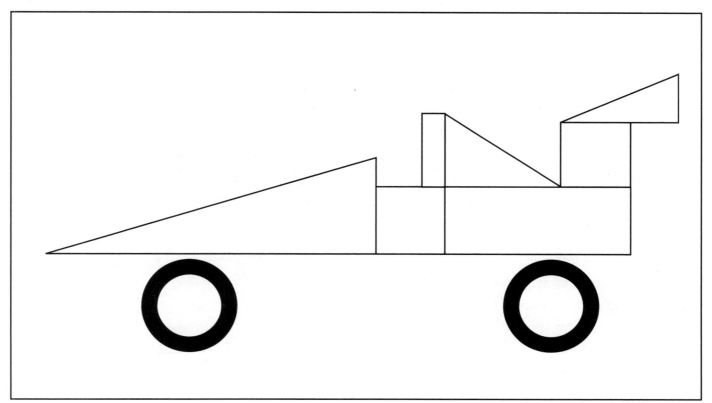

1 **Have a boat race.**

1 **Say the words and trace. Colour the circles.**

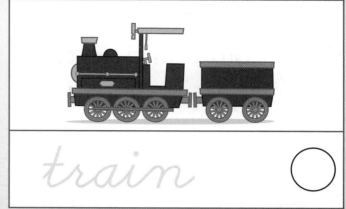

boat ◯

train ◯

car ◯

bike ◯

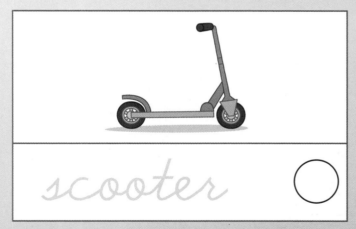

scooter ◯

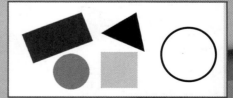

bus ◯

2 **Draw faces.** ☺ ☺ ☹

 ◯
 ◯
 ◯

⑨ Party clothes

1 Colour and describe.

 shirt

 hat

 boots

 shoes

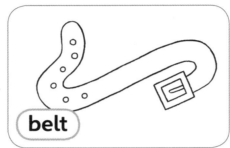 belt

 badge

2 Draw five lines. Guess with your friend.

hat, belt, boots, shirt, badge, shoes

1 Think! **Follow the food and drink.**

I like (biscuits, crisps, salad, sweets). 89

1 Find five differences.

1 Think! **Look and cross out.**

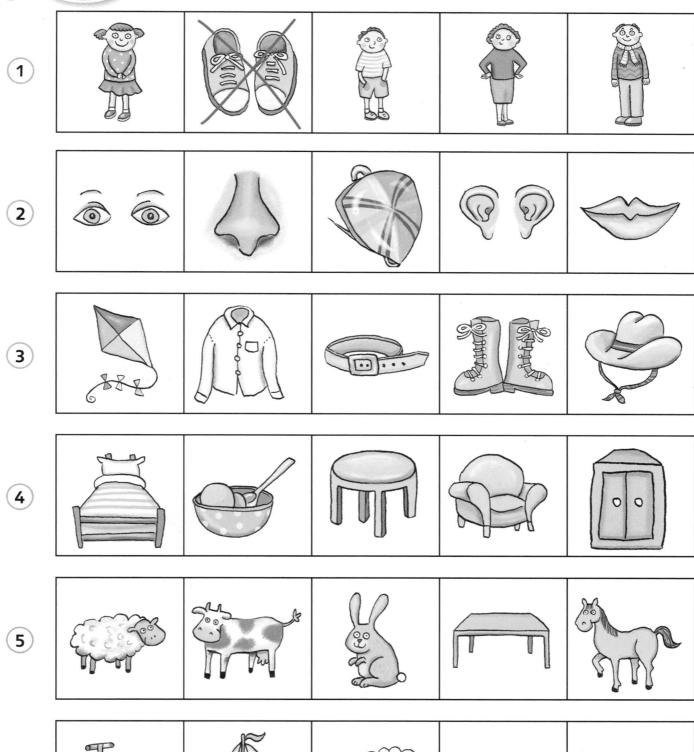

1 Listen and trace.

1

2

3

4

1 **Think! Look and colour.**

1

2

1  **Listen and colour.**

| 1 | 2 | 3 | 4 | 5 | 6 | 7 | 8 | 9 | 10 |

2 Think! **Look and colour.**

1 **Colour. Follow the lines. Describe the uniforms.**

Make a pirate hat.

1 Say the words and trace. Colour the circles.

shirt ◯

hat ◯

boots ◯

shoes ◯

belt ◯

badge ◯

2 Draw faces. ☺ ☺ ☹

 ◯

 ◯

 ◯

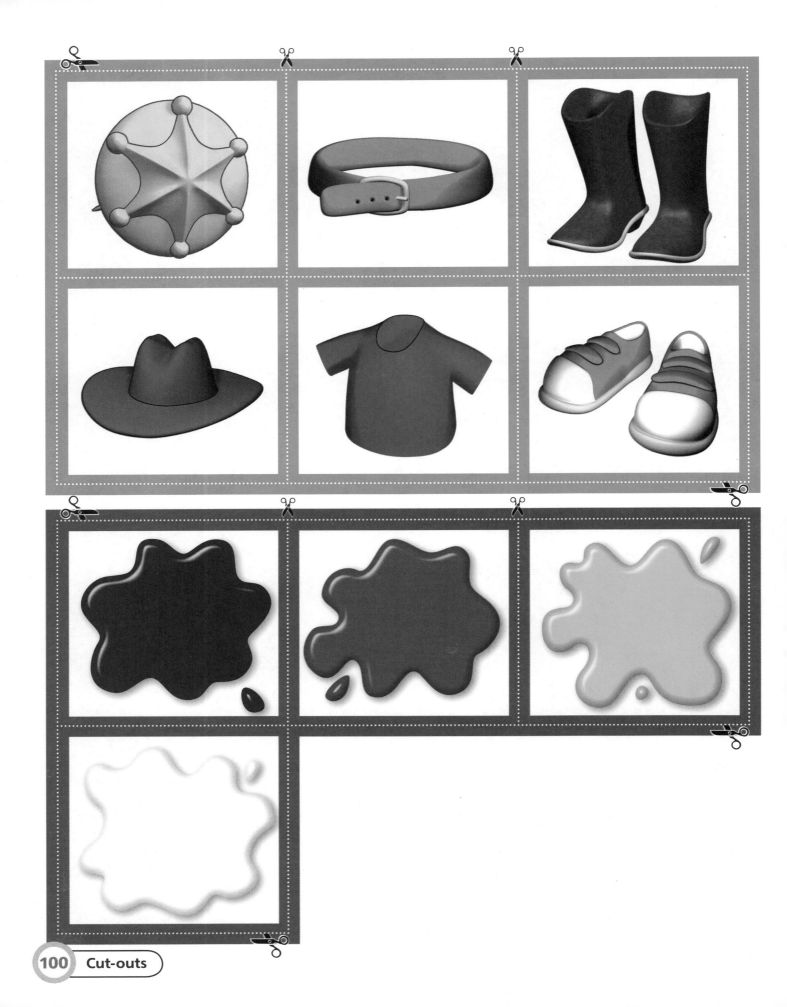

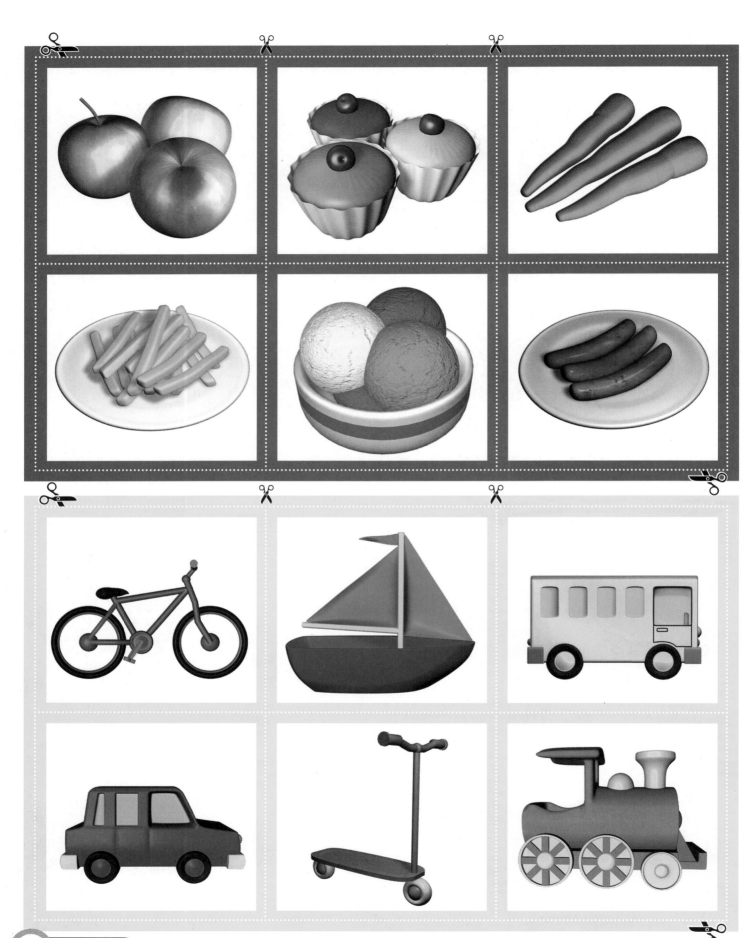

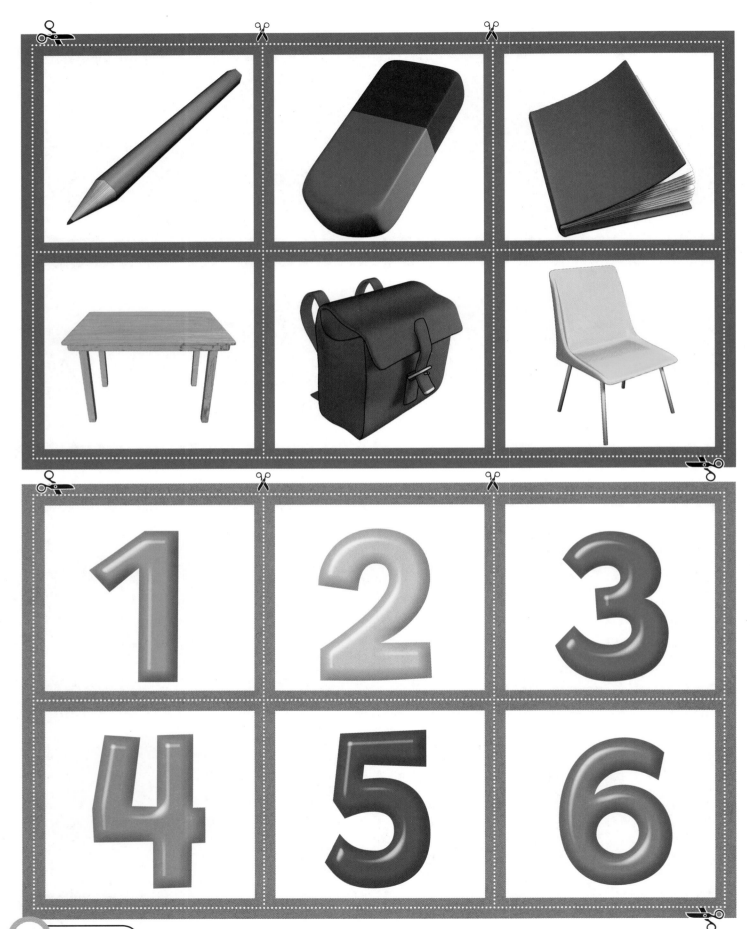

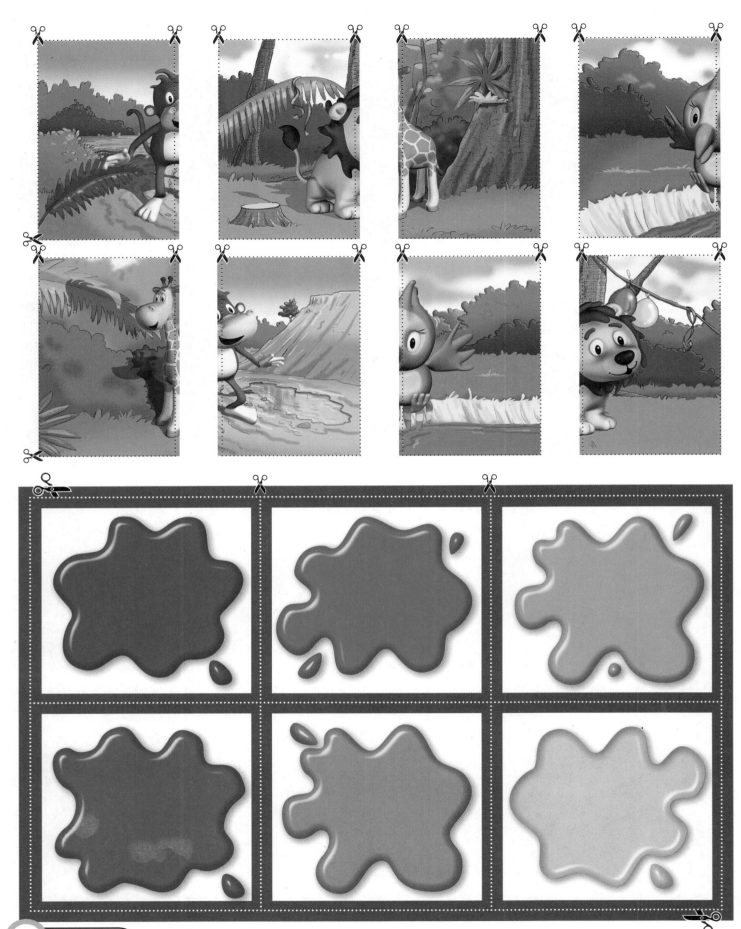